GROSS BUGS™

Locusts

Jonathan Kravetz

The Rosen Publishing Group's

PowerKids Press™

New York

To Fred, who encouraged me to write

Published in 2006 by The Rosen Publishing Group, Inc.
29 East 21st Street, New York, NY 10010

First Edition

Editor: Jennifer Way
Book Design: Ginny Chu

Photo Credits: Cover, pp.1, 9 © Chris Mattison; Frank Lane Picture Agency/Corbis; p. 5 © Reuters/Corbis; p. 5 (inset) © Pierre Holtz/Reuters/Corbis; p. 6 © Academy of Natural Sciences of Philadelphia/Corbis; p. 10 © Gavin G. Thomson; Gallo Images/Corbis; pp. 13, 21 © Patrick Robert/Corbis/Sygma; p.14 © David Aubrey/Corbis; p. 17 © Stephen Dalton/Photo Researchers, Inc.; p. 18 © Paul Zborowski.

Library of Congress Cataloging-in-Publication Data

Kravetz, Jonathan.
Locusts / Jonathan Kravetz.— 1st ed.
    p. cm. — (Gross bugs)
Includes bibliographical references and index.
ISBN 1-4042-3042-4 (library binding)
1. Locusts—Juvenile literature. I. Title. II. Series.

QL508.A2K73 2006
595.7'26—dc22

                                    2004021992

Manufactured in the United States of America

CONTENTS

1. Blotting Out the Sun 4
2. Locusts Around the World..............................7
3. Locusts' Bodies 8
4. What Locusts Eat and What Eats Them 11
5. Locust Eggs 12
6. Nymphs 15
7. Adults 16
8. Mating and Laying Eggs 19
9. How Swarms Affect People 20
10. How People Fight Locusts 22
    Glossary...23
    Index 24
    Web Sites 24

Blotting Out the Sun

Imagine you are a farmer. One day you are out working in your fields. You look up and see the Sun disappearing behind a **swarm** of **insects**! They attack and eat your crops and there is little you can do to stop them. They move on days later. There is nothing left of your crops except dirt and the millions of eggs the insects laid in your soil. Your farm was just attacked by locusts.

Locusts have troubled farmers around the world for centuries. There are thousands of **species** of locusts. Locusts can be found in nearly every country.

Locusts belong to a **family** of insects called Acrididae. They are similar to grasshoppers but with one major difference. When conditions are right, some species of locusts will gather in large numbers, forming a swarm.

The farmer above is walking through his field, which is being attacked by a swarm of locusts. A swarm is often made up of millions, or even billions, of locusts. After the swarm has eaten the crops, the females will lay their eggs in the ground. This produces millions more locusts. *Inset:* This is a close-up of a swarm in Senegal, where locusts destroyed crops in 2004.

These pictures of locusts were created around 1700. Locusts have troubled farmers for centuries. Farmers in the nineteenth-century United States lived through swarms of the Rocky Mountain locust. This species died out around 1900.

6

Locusts Around the World

Giant swarms of locusts have been destroying crops for thousands of years. Locust swarms have occurred almost everywhere in the world. There were no locust swarms in North America or Europe during the last century. This was due to weather changes and the extinction, or dying out, of several species. Locusts still swarm in Africa, Asia, and Australia. An outbreak in Asia in 1999 covered 6,000 square miles (15,540 sq km)!

Only about a dozen of the locust species swarm. Luckily the ones that swarm do not swarm that often. Most species are **solitary** and only come together to **mate**. When food is limited, locusts can change into a swarming **phase** called the **migratory** phase. In this phase they travel in a swarm to search for food.

Locusts' Bodies

Locusts range in size from ½ inch to 6 inches (1 cm–15 cm) long. Their color varies from green to brown. Adult locusts have a head, a **thorax**, and an **abdomen**. They have four wings and a stiff outer shell called an exoskeleton. Locusts have two **antennae** they use to sense what is around them. Locusts have five eyes, which include two larger eyes that sit on either side of their head. They also have one eye on each antenna and one between the antennae. Locusts' ears are on their abdomens.

The locust's mouth consists of a number of parts. The locust has lips, a tongue, and two sets of jaws. It wets its food with saliva, or spit, and chews it with its mouth. A locust's rear legs are longer and stronger than its two other sets of legs. These rear legs make them powerful jumpers.

This is a desert locust from South Africa. The color of a locust can depend on the weather where the locust lives. Dry places tend to produce more tan and brown locusts. Green locusts tend to live in wetter areas. The locusts' color helps it match its surroundings. This is known as camouflage.

9

Many animals eat locusts, such as this bird. Farmers in the 1800s found that their chickens liked to eat locusts. These farmers later discovered that they could not eat the eggs or the meat from these chickens. The locusts made them taste terrible!

What Locusts Eat and What Eats Them

Locusts are not picky eaters. Swarming locusts will eat any plants in their path. They will eat corn, cotton, fruit, and vegetables. Locusts will also eat leather, cloth, paper, wool, and even dead locusts when they are really hungry! Locusts at both the **nymph** and adult stages can eat crops until there is nothing left. In their migratory phase, nymphs move together in groups called bands to search for food. Groups of migratory adults are called swarms.

Many animals eat locusts, including birds, other insects, and lizards. Some farmers in China train ducks to eat locusts to help reduce the number of these gross bugs.

A single locust swarm can eat as much food as do several thousand people in one day!

Locust Eggs

The life cycle of locusts has three stages, which are egg, nymph, and adult. The time locusts spend in each stage depends on the species. It can even be different within a single species, because the weather can greatly affect when locusts mate.

Female locusts lay from 20 to 100 eggs at a time. These eggs are laid in the ground in a group called an egg pod. It is held together by a sticky matter made by the female. The egg pod is 1 to 1½ inches (2.5–4 cm) long. One female can usually lay only three egg pods in her lifetime.

Eggs grow at different speeds. They can take between 10 days and 12 months to grow. For example, warm weather tends to cause the eggs to grow faster.

This is the egg pod of an African locust. The female locust lays egg pods in the ground. The eggs are held together in an egg pod by a sticky gum that helps keep the eggs dry. Egg pods are usually laid in large groups called egg beds.

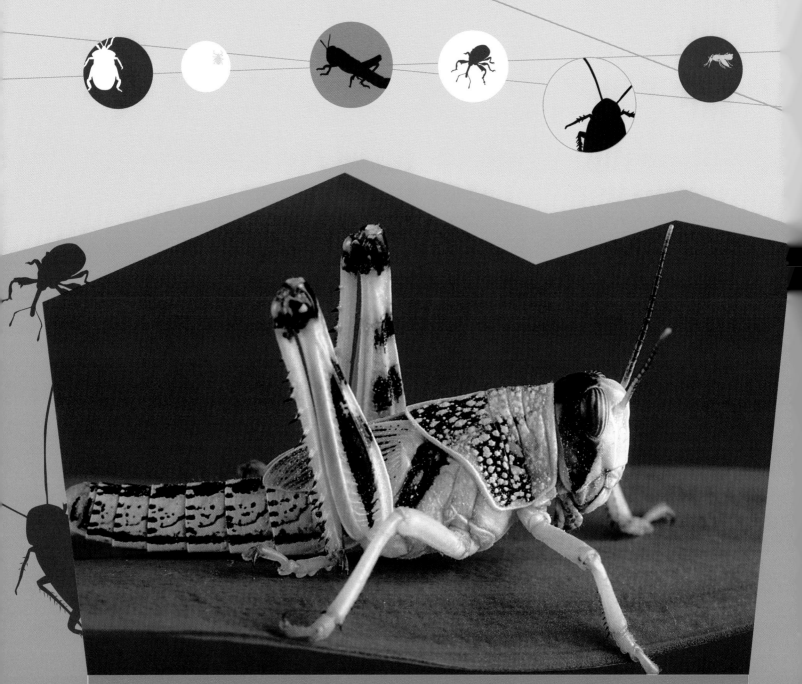

Locust nymphs, such as the one above, cannot fly. Their wings are too small. With each molt the nymphs' bodies grow and their wings get larger. All the nymphs from an egg pod usually hatch on the same morning. It usually takes about three days for the whole egg bed to hatch.

Nymphs

The young locust is called a nymph. When the nymph is ready to hatch, it bursts out of the egg pod. It then crawls above ground with the help of a sack at the base of its neck. It sheds a thin, white skin when it reaches the surface and then waits while its new skin hardens.

Nymphs grow by **molting**. When the nymph molts, it sheds its old skin and has a new, softer skin underneath. The nymph grows a bit longer before its new skin hardens. With each molt the nymph grows and its wings get bigger. Molting usually occurs five times. The new adult is called a fledgling. Adult locusts do not molt.

The desert locust (*Schistocerca gregaria*) is one of the most common locusts on Earth. The first nymph stage of the desert locust lasts around 5 days. The second stage lasts 6 days, the third lasts 7 days. The fourth lasts 8 days, and the fifth lasts 12 days.

After the final molt, the fledgling has fully formed wings. It takes about a week before they harden. Until then the locust can fly only short distances. The fledgling adult cannot yet mate.

The amount of time before a fledgling becomes a fully **mature** adult depends on how much food and water is available. When there is little food or water and cold weather, an adult may take as long as six months to mature, or grow up. Male locusts start to mature first. Then they give off a chemical from their skin that signals females to begin maturing.

The length of a locust's life depends on how long it takes to mature. The faster a locust grows and mates, the shorter its life.

Adult locusts have fully formed wings and can fly. Scientists are not sure what causes solitary locusts to enter the migratory, or swarming, phase. Scientists think that the weather and a lack of food have something to do with it.

These female locusts are laying eggs. They use the egg-laying tube at the end of their abdomen to push holes into the soft dirt. They will lay their eggs into this hole and then leave a sticky matter on top of the eggs to guard them. During the egg laying a female locust's abdomen gets about twice as long as normal.

Mating and Laying Eggs

Adult locusts usually begin mating in spring and can mate throughout the summer. Male locusts make sounds to draw females to them. The process of making sounds is called **stridulating**. It occurs when locusts rub a rear leg against their front wing. When the male and female meet, they touch the tips of their abdomens. Then the male **fertilizes** the female's eggs.

Not long after mating, the female locust lays her eggs. She feels for soft, warm soil with the tip of her abdomen. Then the female locust finds the right place for her eggs. She pushes the egg-laying tube, called an ovipositor, at the end of her abdomen into the soil and makes a hole. Then she lays her eggs. The acts of mating and laying the eggs take 1 to 2 hours.

How Swarms Affect People

Locusts are one of the most harmful crop-eating insects on Earth. There have been records of locust swarms throughout recorded history. When locusts eat all the crops in a country, there can be a **famine**. The worst swarm in the history of the United States occurred in the 1870s and passed through states including Nebraska and Colorado. Today, however, there are no swarming locusts in the United States. The Rocky Mountain locust, the only swarming species in North America, died out around 1900.

Locusts continue to swarm in many countries around the world. Some African countries, like Sudan, are more in danger than other places. They often do not have enough money for **pesticides**, which can be used to fight locusts.

These airplanes are spraying pesticides to kill swarms of locusts in Africa. The longest recorded locust swarm occurred in East Africa between 1950 and 1962. It is thought that there were around 40 million locusts for every square mile (sq km). That adds up to more than five billion locusts!

How People Fight Locusts

Early American settlers tried many methods to guard their crops from locusts. Some settlers dragged a flat pan filled with kerosene or hot tar through **infested** fields. The locusts would hop onto the pans and fry!

People used to believe that locusts brought illness with them. When locusts die in large numbers, the piles of rotting locusts produce a terrible smell. Some people used to believe that this odor caused human beings to get sick. We now know, however, that these terrible odors do not cause illness.

Today people fight locusts with pesticides. These can be useful for saving crops, although it is hard to wipe out all the locusts. In many places, such as Africa, Asia, and Australia, swarming locusts remain a danger to crops.

GLOSSARY

abdomen (AB-duh-min) The large, rear part of an insect's body.

antennae (an-TEH-nee) Thin, rodlike parts used to feel things, located on the heads of certain animals.

family (FAM-lee) The scientific name for a large group of plants or animals that are alike in some ways.

famine (FA-min) A shortage of food that causes people to go hungry.

fertilizes (FUR-tuh-lyz-ez) Puts male cells inside a female to make babies.

infested (in-FEST-ed) Spread over an area in a troublesome manner.

insects (IN-sekts) Small creatures that often have six legs and wings.

mate (MAYT) To join together to make babies.

mature (muh-TOOR) Full-grown.

migratory (MY-gruh-tor-ee) Having to do with moving from one place to another.

molting (MOHLT-ing) Shedding hair, feathers, shell, horns, or skin.

nymph (NIMF) A young insect that has not yet grown into an adult.

pesticides (PES-tih-sydz) Poisons used to kill pests.

phase (FAYZ) Different stage of life.

solitary (SAH-lih-ter-ee) Spending most time alone.

species (SPEE-sheez) A single kind of living thing. All people are one species.

stridulating (STRID-yoo-layt-ing) Rubbing a leg against a wing, creating a buzzing sound.

swarm (SWORM) A large number of insects, often in motion.

thorax (THOR-aks) The middle part of the body of an insect.

INDEX

A
abdomen, 8, 19
Acrididae, 4
antennae, 8

B
bands, 11

E
egg pod, 12, 15
egg(s), 4, 12, 19

exoskeleton, 8

F
fledgling, 15–16

L
legs, 8, 19

M
mating, 7, 12, 16,
   19

N
nymph(s), 11, 15

P
pesticides, 20, 22

S
species, 4, 7, 12
stridulating, 19
swarm(s), 4, 7, 11,
   20

Web Sites
Due to the changing nature of Internet links, PowerKids Press has
developed an online list of Web sites related to the subject of this book.
This site is updated regularly. Please use this link to access the list:
www.powerkidslinks.com/gbugs/locusts/